EXPLORE
THE PARTHENON

AN ANCIENT GREEK TEMPLE AND ITS SCULPTURES

Ian Jenkins   Kate Morton

THE BRITISH MUSEUM PRESS

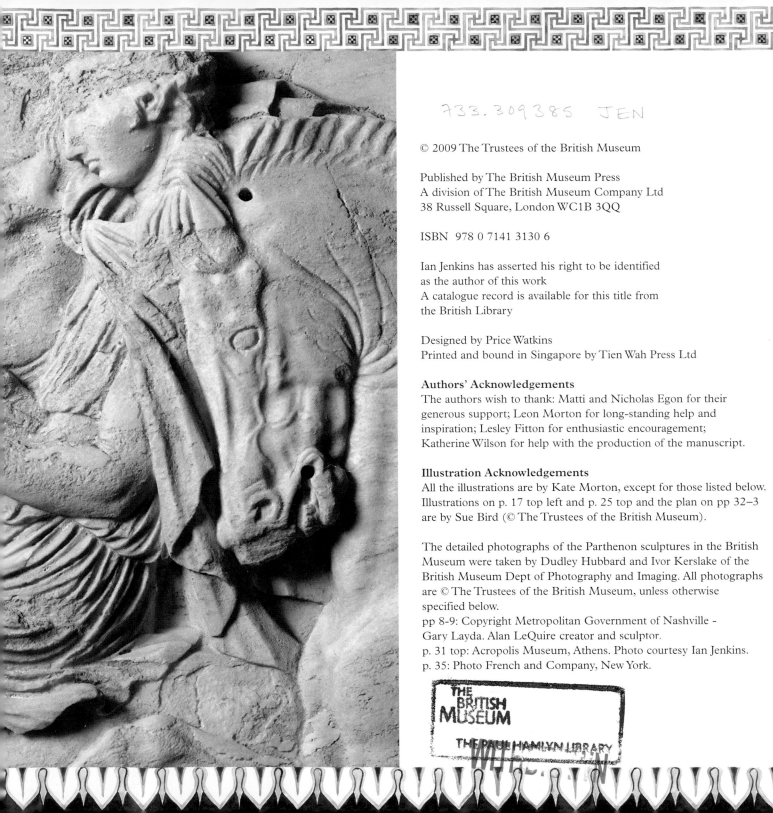

© 2009 The Trustees of the British Museum

Published by The British Museum Press
A division of The British Museum Company Ltd
38 Russell Square, London WC1B 3QQ

ISBN 978 0 7141 3130 6

Ian Jenkins has asserted his right to be identified
as the author of this work
A catalogue record is available for this title from
the British Library

Designed by Price Watkins
Printed and bound in Singapore by Tien Wah Press Ltd

Authors' Acknowledgements
The authors wish to thank: Matti and Nicholas Egon for their
generous support; Leon Morton for long-standing help and
inspiration; Lesley Fitton for enthusiastic encouragement;
Katherine Wilson for help with the production of the manuscript.

Illustration Acknowledgements
All the illustrations are by Kate Morton, except for those listed below.
Illustrations on p. 17 top left and p. 25 top and the plan on pp 32–3
are by Sue Bird (© The Trustees of the British Museum).

The detailed photographs of the Parthenon sculptures in the British
Museum were taken by Dudley Hubbard and Ivor Kerslake of the
British Museum Dept of Photography and Imaging. All photographs
are © The Trustees of the British Museum, unless otherwise
specified below.
pp 8-9: Copyright Metropolitan Government of Nashville -
Gary Layda. Alan LeQuire creator and sculptor.
p. 31 top: Acropolis Museum, Athens. Photo courtesy Ian Jenkins.
p. 35: Photo French and Company, New York.

CONTENTS

A Greek Temple 4

Building the Parthenon 6

The Statue Inside the Temple 8

Sculptures on the Outside of the Temple 10

Carving the Frieze 16

The Panathenaic Festival 18

The Horsemen 24

The Chariot Race 26

Worshippers on Foot 28

The Gods 30

A Plan of the Procession shown
in the Parthenon Frieze 32

Destruction and Rescue 34

Further Reading 36

Index 36

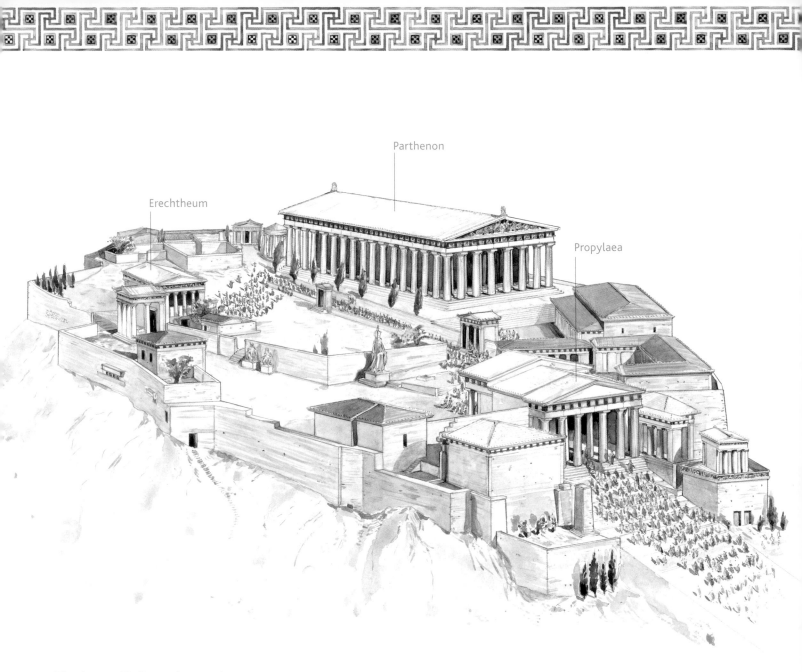

Erechtheum

Parthenon

Propylaea

The Acropolis from the north-west.

A GREEK TEMPLE

At the centre of the modern city of Athens in Greece there is a rocky hill or Acropolis. The word means 'high city'. Here, two and a half thousand years ago, the Athenians built a temple which came to be known as the Parthenon.

THE Acropolis was fortified with strong walls and could be entered only through a great gateway or Propylaea. Once inside, the visitor to the ancient Acropolis would have seen the Parthenon and also other temples and shrines. Around these, there were many sculptures set up in honour of the gods. There was also a great altar at which animals were sacrificed, and where worshippers would gather. People did not assemble inside a Greek temple to worship, unlike a Muslim mosque or a Christian church. The purpose of the temple was to provide a shelter for a statue of the god or goddess. The Parthenon housed a colossal statue of the goddess Athena Parthenos. In ancient Greek Parthenos means 'virgin'.

The Parthenon had two separate rooms. Massive bronze doors led into each room. The largest room faced east and contained the statue. The smaller room was entered from the west. This was a treasury for precious gold and silver.

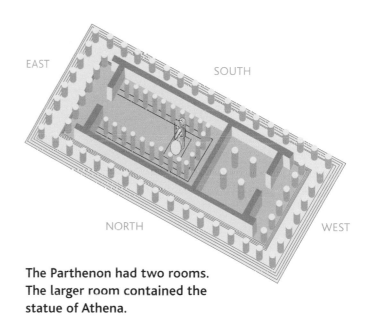

EAST
SOUTH
NORTH
WEST

The Parthenon had two rooms. The larger room contained the statue of Athena.

5

BUILDING THE PARTHENON

The Parthenon was built between 447 and 432 BC. It was made of expensive white marble – even the roof tiles. In its day it was the largest temple ever built in mainland Greece.

AT the time that the Parthenon was built, Athens was a democracy. This means that all male citizens could help to pass laws and decide how Athens was governed. (Slaves and women were not citizens and did not take part.) Perikles was a leading politician. He oversaw the building of several temples in and around Athens, including the Parthenon. The Parthenon was the grandest and the most expensive of all. It measures some 69.51 metres (228 feet) long and 30.86 metres (101 feet) wide.

The great quantity of marble needed to build the Parthenon had to be brought from Mount Pentelikon, some sixteen kilometres (10 miles) outside the city. This marble was worked with such perfection that the joint between two blocks is finer than a human hair.

The Parthenon is famous for its 'refinements'. These include the inward lean of the walls and columns. Perhaps most remarkable of all is the way that the floor and other horizontal surfaces in the temple were made to curve gently upwards. This drawing exaggerates the curves to show how the 'refinements' work. They make the building look very pleasing to the eye, almost as if it is a living thing.

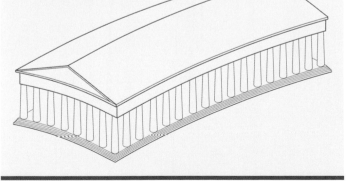

The Athenians used a wooden crane to lift the sculptures and heavy blocks of marble.

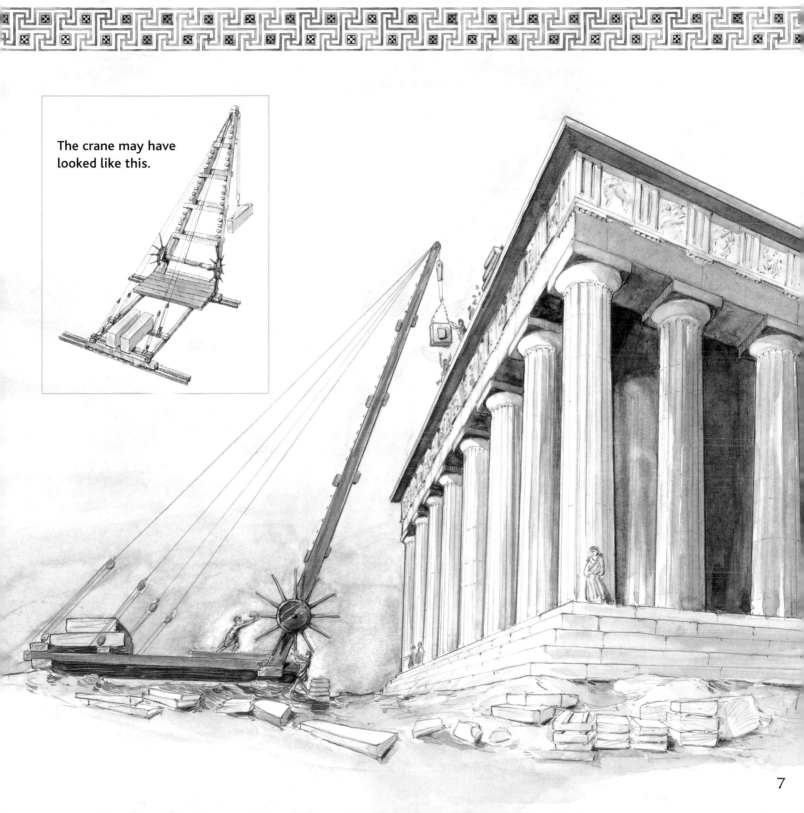

The crane may have looked like this.

THE STATUE INSIDE THE TEMPLE

Inside the Parthenon stood a colossal statue of Athena Parthenos, 'Athena the virgin'. It was made of gold and ivory by Pheidias, one of the greatest of all ancient Greek sculptors.

THE statue, with its base, stood over 12 metres (40 feet) high. First the sculptor built a wooden framework. On this he hung sheets of gold for the dress and armour, and ivory for the skin of the face, arms and feet. Such statues are called *chryselephantine*. Chrysos means 'gold' in ancient Greek.

Athena was a warrior goddess and she is shown with a helmet, shield and spear. Inside the shield coiled a protective snake. Athena held the shield with one hand, and with the other she supported a statue of the winged goddess of victory, Nike. On her breast Athena wore the *aegis*. This was a poncho-like garment, decorated with a fringe of snakes. At its centre was the face of the gorgon, Medusa. The inner and outer surfaces of the shield and the soles of Athena's sandals were carved or painted with scenes of mythical battles. The marble base on which the great statue stood was worked to show the Olympian gods gathered to watch Athena and the smith-god Hephaistos making Pandora. According to Greek mythology Pandora was the first woman.

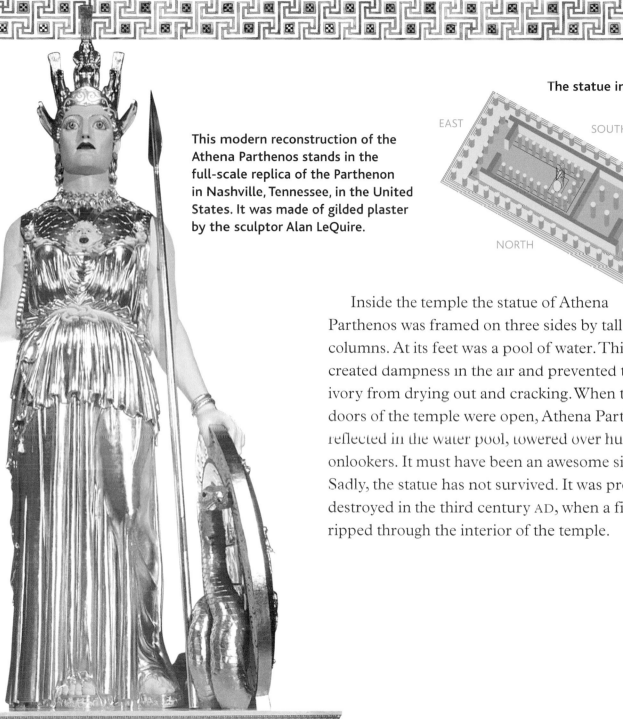

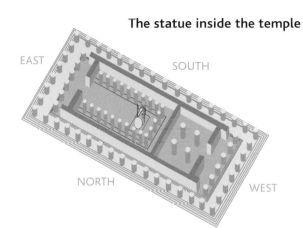

The statue inside the temple

EAST

SOUTH

NORTH

WEST

This modern reconstruction of the Athena Parthenos stands in the full-scale replica of the Parthenon in Nashville, Tennessee, in the United States. It was made of gilded plaster by the sculptor Alan LeQuire.

Inside the temple the statue of Athena Parthenos was framed on three sides by tall columns. At its feet was a pool of water. This created dampness in the air and prevented the ivory from drying out and cracking. When the doors of the temple were open, Athena Parthenos, reflected in the water pool, towered over human onlookers. It must have been an awesome sight. Sadly, the statue has not survived. It was probably destroyed in the third century AD, when a fire ripped through the interior of the temple.

9

SCULPTURES ON THE OUTSIDE OF THE TEMPLE

As well as the statue of Athena inside the Parthenon, marble sculptures decorated the outside. There are three different types: metopes, pediments and frieze.

METOPES are rectangular panels that were slotted into place to form a frieze above the columns on the outside of the temple. There were ninety-two metopes. They showed scenes of mythical battles – a different one on each side of the temple.

The sculptures from the south side have survived best and these show a fight between human Lapiths and centaurs (mythical creatures who are part-man, part-horse). They tell the story of the disastrous wedding feast of the Lapith king, Perithoos. The centaurs were invited guests, but they became drunk with wine and tried to carry off the Lapith women. Each metope is carved with a Lapith and a centaur, usually fighting. Sometimes a centaur tries to gallop away with a Lapith girl, who struggles to get free from his grip.

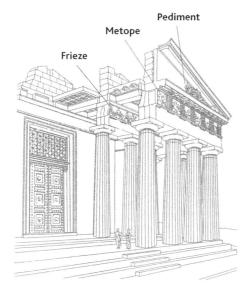

The sculptures on the outside of the temple.

A hand grips the hair of a centaur. He grimaces with pain and rage.

PEDIMENTS are the triangles formed by the sloping roof of a temple, one at either end. The bottom of this triangle provided a shallow shelf, on which were placed sculptures. In the case of the Parthenon, the pediment sculptures were carved as full, solid figures, even though they could only be seen from the front.

The west pediment showed a story from the life of the goddess Athena. It was the contest between her and Poseidon, god of the sea, for the city of Athens and its countryside. The gods raced to the Acropolis in chariots. Then each performed a miracle watched by judges and other witnesses on either side. Poseidon struck the rock with his trident and produced a salt-water spring. Athena brought forth the first olive tree, and this was judged the greater gift.

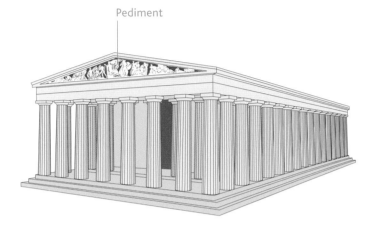

Pediment

The west pediment of the Parthenon showed the contest between Athena and Poseidon.

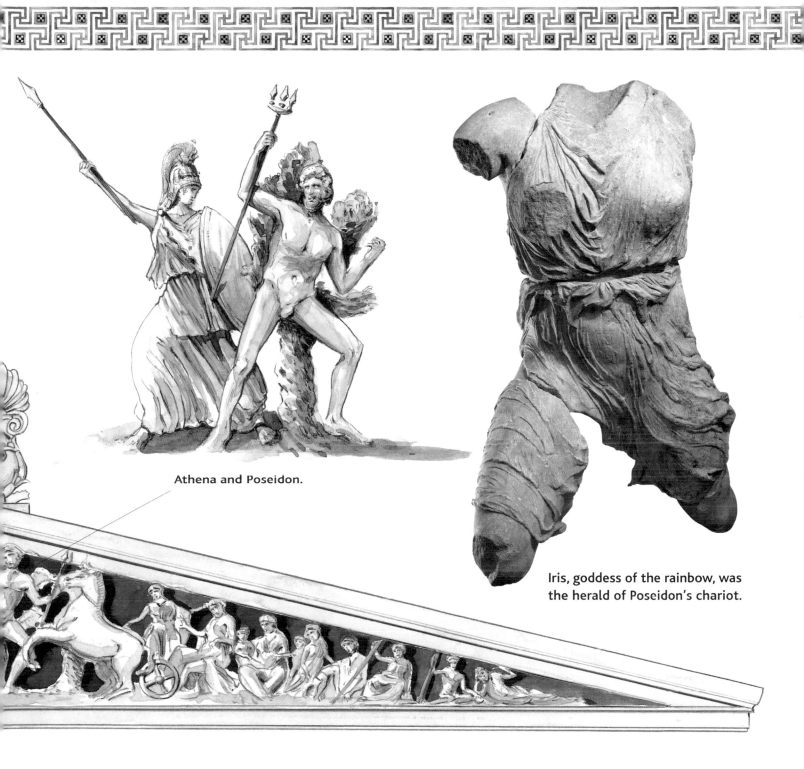

Athena and Poseidon.

Iris, goddess of the rainbow, was the herald of Poseidon's chariot.

13

THE east pediment showed the birth of Athena. Greek stories tell how Athena sprang, fully grown-up, from the head of her father Zeus. The sculptures themselves are missing, but we can imagine Zeus seated, while Athena strides out fully grown and armed. Her brother Hephaistos will also have been present. It was Hephaistos who cut open Zeus' head with an axe to release his brain child. On either side there were sculptures of other gods. Finally, in one corner of the pediment, the chariot of the sun god Helios rose out of the sea at dawn; while in the other corner, the chariot of the moon goddess Selene sank beneath the horizon.

The god of wine, Dionysos, from the east pediment.

14

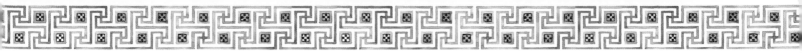

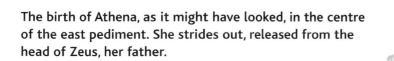

The birth of Athena, as it might have looked, in the centre of the east pediment. She strides out, released from the head of Zeus, her father.

The horse of the moon goddess Selene, weary after its night's work.

CARVING THE FRIEZE

The Parthenon frieze ran for 160 metres (524 feet) around all four sides of the building. It shows the procession of the Panathenaic Festival, which took place in Athens every year.

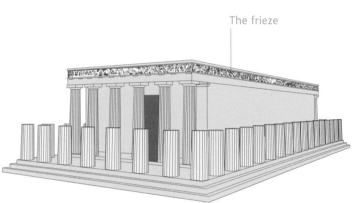

The frieze

THE frieze was carved into blocks of stone that had already been set in place on the building. Unlike the metopes, the depth of carving in the frieze is very shallow. Yet the frieze still manages to show many figures, sometimes seven or eight abreast. It is a marvellous achievement of the carvers. A plan of the procession must have been drawn up to show the carvers what to do. (You can see a plan on pages 32–33.)

As well as carving the marble, the sculptors added metal details, such as the bridles and reins of the horses. There were no stirrups, because these had not been invented.

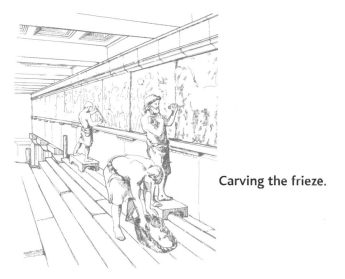

Carving the frieze.

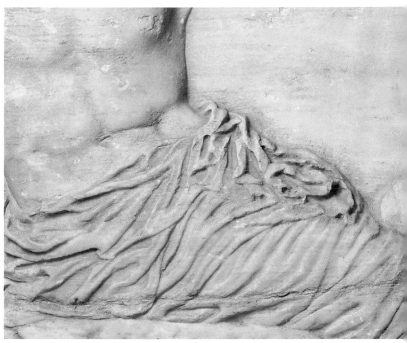

The details of the frieze are fully carved, even though the frieze was high up on the building and never seen close-up. The faces, bodies and clothing look real and alive.

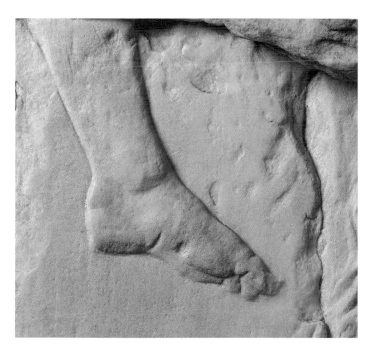

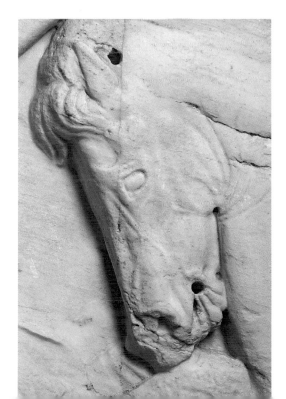

THE PANATHENAIC FESTIVAL

The Athenian year was full of religious festivals honouring the gods. The most important gods lived on Mount Olympos, where they were ruled by Zeus. The Panathenaic Festival was held at the height of summer and celebrated the birth of Athena.

PAN in ancient Greek means 'all', and everybody in Athens could take part in this Festival. There were competitions in music and athletics. On the last day of the Festival a great procession made its way to the Acropolis. In the cool of the early morning it gathered at the city gate. At the signal it began to move off, marching along the straight road that led into the market place or *agora*. With the procession there went a model of a ship that moved on rollers. As if it were a sail, a newly woven robe or *peplos* was displayed on the mast. It was worked as a tapestry and showed a mythical battle between Olympian gods and giants. This *peplos* was for Athena's statue.

Jars of olive oil were given as prizes at the Panathenaic Games. One side of this jar shows victorious athletes dancing. The other side shows Athena. The Greek writing beside her says 'I am one of the prizes from the games at Athens'.

PASSING through the market place, the procession climbed the slopes of the Acropolis until it reached the great gateway or Propylaea. This marvellous building was put up shortly after the Parthenon was built. The people in the procession paused and waited their turn to file through the central passage of the Propylaea.

The wooden statue was so old that the Athenians thought that it fell from the sky at the beginning of time. It showed Athena Polias or 'protector of the city'. It was kept in the Erectheum, a temple built on the north side of the Acropolis. Athena's statue stood in the east room of this temple. When the doors were open, the goddess could see the great altar in front of the temple. Here a hundred cattle were sacrificed and their meat eaten at a great feast that marked the end of the Panathenaic Festival.

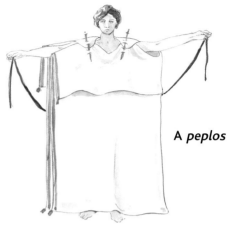

A *peplos*

As they did so, they could turn and look back over the city below and the sea beyond.

The *peplos* was not taken to the great gold and ivory statue of Athena standing in the Parthenon. Instead, it was presented to a much older, smaller image of Athena that was made of olive wood.

Left: The Propylaea or gateway
Above: The Erechtheum

In the frieze,
a priest and a
child hold up the
folded *peplos*.

21

The Panathenaic procession is shown in the Parthenon frieze, which runs right round the temple.

WHEN the ancient Greeks chose a subject for the decorative sculpture of a temple, they usually took a story about gods or heroes from Greek myth. This is what they did for the pediments and metopes of the Parthenon. So it is surprising to find the Athenians themselves shown in the Parthenon frieze. These human beings are not really portraits of ordinary people. Instead, they are shown as an ideal community. The Athenians of Perikles' day wanted to be remembered at their best by generations to come.

The procession shown in the frieze is made up of different groups. There are male and female,

young and old, citizens and non-citizens, animals and humans, gods and mortals. Like the Panathenaic Festival itself, the frieze aimed to include the whole city. However, not everybody who was shown in the frieze could have taken part in the actual procession. For example, chariots could not possibly have raced among the people and cattle walking. The chariots must have held their contest at a different time and place. They were included in the frieze, however, because they make a good picture. The same is true of the mounted horsemen. The actual procession contained foot soldiers, but the cavalry look much more exciting on the frieze.

Young men are bringing cattle to sacrifice.

THE HORSEMEN

While the Parthenon was being built, Perikles increased the number of the Athenian cavalry from a fighting force of three hundred to one of a thousand. The thrilling spectacle of the cavalcade in the frieze captures the excitement that Athenians must have felt on seeing their new cavalry on parade. There were sixty horsemen on each of the long sides of the temple, cleverly overlapped in ranks.

In a carving that is only a few centimetres deep, the sculptors show a rank of seven horsemen side by side. The diagram shows the riders as we see them in the frieze itself and as we would see them if we were looking down on them from above.

The horses once had bridles and reins made of bronze. You can see the holes where the bridles were fixed.

The background of the frieze was probably painted blue to make the carved figures stand out clearly. Colour was also used on the figures.

25

THE CHARIOT RACE

When the Parthenon was built, the ancient Greeks no longer used chariots in war. Chariot-racing, however, was a thrilling event in the athletic games of the Panathenaic Festival.

THE chariot race included a race on foot. Two people rode together in the chariot. There was a charioteer, holding the reins, and a foot-soldier (*hoplite*). When the chariot reached a marker, the foot-soldier would leap down and, wearing full armour, he dashed to a finishing line. The first one to cross the line was the winner.

The chariot race appears in the long north and south friezes, ahead of the mounted horsemen. Sadly, many blocks from this part of the frieze were damaged or lost in the explosion that destroyed the Parthenon in 1687 (see page 34). The lightweight racing chariots were each drawn by four horses. The drivers wear long tunics. The soldiers' helmets are pushed back on their heads to reveal their faces. The horse-hair crests of these helmets often fly in the wind and echo the billowing cloaks. Each soldier grips a large round shield with one hand, while the other hand grasps the guard rail of the chariot.

A painted water-jar showing a chariot being harnessed.

Four galloping horses, manes flickering, pull a chariot with a foot-soldier and a driver. The driver's figure is now almost broken away.

WORSHIPPERS ON FOOT

Various groups of figures walk ahead of the chariots. They are making their way towards the gods, who are waiting to receive the offerings they are bringing.

AHEAD of the chariots are bearded elders. In front of them walk musicians and, ahead of them, youths carrying water-jars. Youths carrying trays of offerings appear next and they walk behind sheep and cattle being led as sacrificial victims. Around the corner, on the east frieze, girls or women appear for the first time.

Girls walk in the procession.

tray-bearer   water-carriers   musicians

At the head of the procession are men who are not actually taking part, but waiting for the procession to arrive. Standing and leaning on sticks, these men talk among themselves. They are, perhaps, officials waiting for the procession to reach the Acropolis. Or they may be heroes of Athenian legend.

elders

29

THE GODS

The Panathenaic Festival was a time for flattering the gods with prayers and presents.

THE ancient Greeks imagined their gods to be very like human beings. They were larger than life, had supernatural powers and did not suffer death, but in other ways they were like us. They were highly competitive and could be jealous of one another and of humans. The gods were unreliable, and it was important to get them on your side. Pride of place in the centre of the east frieze, therefore, was given to the gods. They are shown seated like a grandstand audience waiting for the procession to arrive and the sacrifices to begin.

Because they sit, the gods and goddesses appear larger than the standing and walking figures of the frieze. Each has his or her own personality. Often some object provides a clue to who they are. Hermes, a messenger god, sits watching and waiting and has a sun hat (*petasos*) on his knee. Demeter, the goddess of the fertile earth, holds a bundle of corn stems. Hephaistos, the lame smith of the gods, supports his right side with a crutch under his right armpit.

The gods are arranged in two groups, one facing the southern branch of the procession,

Hermes   Dionysos   Demeter   Ares   Iris   Hera   Zeus

the other the northern branch. Between them are five figures – two adults and three children – who are involved in a ceremony with the *peplos* for Athena's statue. A priest in a long robe and a child hold this folded blanket of woollen cloth.

Poseidon, Apollo and Artemis wait for the ceremonies to begin.

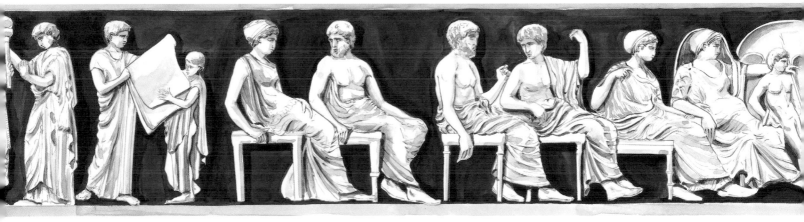

The *peplos*   Athena   Hephaistos   Poseidon   Apollo   Artemis   Aphrodite Eros

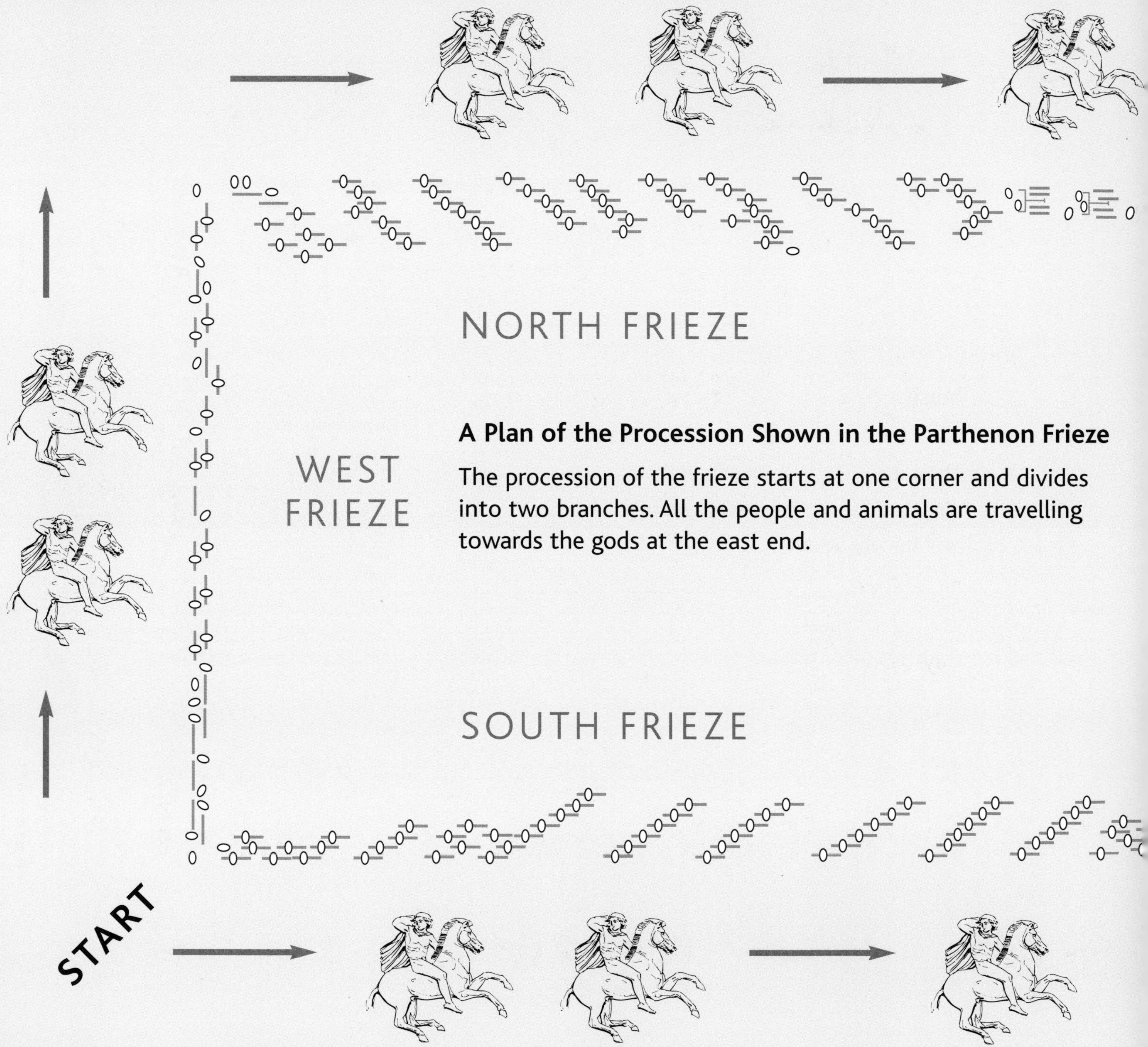

NORTH FRIEZE

WEST
FRIEZE

A Plan of the Procession Shown in the Parthenon Frieze

The procession of the frieze starts at one corner and divides into two branches. All the people and animals are travelling towards the gods at the east end.

SOUTH FRIEZE

START

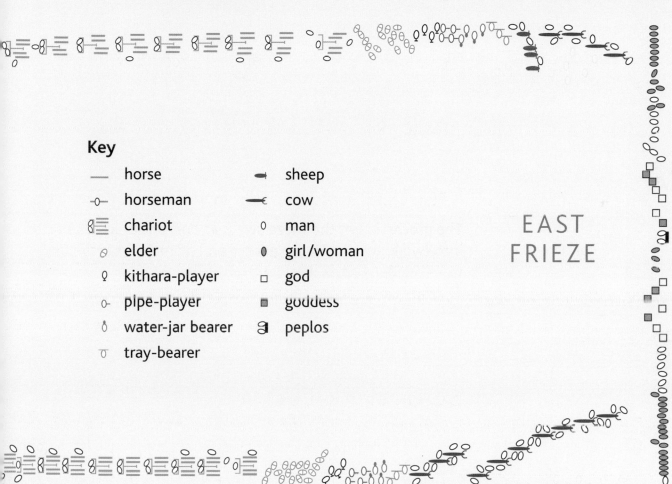

Key

—	horse	◗	sheep
⊸	horseman	≺	cow
⬚	chariot	○	man
⊘	elder	◐	girl/woman
♀	kithara-player	☐	god
⊶	pipe-player	⬛	goddess
◊	water-jar bearer	⧢	peplos
�	tray-bearer		

EAST
FRIEZE

33

DESTRUCTION AND RESCUE

THE Parthenon has had a long history and, over the years, its purpose has changed more than once. Around AD 500, it was turned into a church for Christian worship. Nearly a thousand years later it became a mosque for the Ottoman Turks who ruled Greece as part of their empire.

The biggest change came about in 1687. In that year an Italian General from Venice, Francesco Morosini, besieged the Turkish garrison on the Acropolis. The Turks had stored gunpowder in the Parthenon, and their families had taken refuge within its strong walls. A bomb from one of Morosini's guns came through the roof of the temple and ignited the gunpowder. The explosion, and the fire that followed, killed everybody in it. The roof was blown off and the central walls and columns were brought down. From this time on the Parthenon was a ruin.

In 1798 Lord Elgin, a Scottish nobleman, was sent to Constantinople (modern Istanbul) as Britain's ambassador to Turkey. At this time Greece was still a part of the Turkish Empire and Lord Elgin was especially interested in the remains of ancient Greece. He gathered together a group of artists and scholars and sent them to study the ancient buildings on the Acropolis of Athens. The Parthenon stood in ruins and a little mosque had been built on its ancient marble floor.

Lord Elgin.

The Parthenon is blown up in 1687.

Every day the Parthenon suffered further damage, and its marble sculptures were being lost at an alarming rate. Elgin and his team decided to save as many of the sculptures as could be removed from the building. These were acquired by the British Museum in 1816. Others remained in Athens and are now in the Acropolis Museum.

After the explosion in 1687 the Parthenon was a ruin. A small mosque was built inside.

FURTHER READING

Ian Jenkins, *An Athenian Childhood*, Joint Association of Classical Teachers Illustrated Monograph 2, 1979.
Steven G. Miller and Athena Stamatis, *Plato at Olympia*, Lucy Braggiotti Editions Athens 2008.
Alexandra Villing, *The Ancient Greeks: Their Lives and Their World*, British Museum Press forthcoming.
Richard Woff, *Pocket Explorer: The Ancient Greek World*, British Museum Press 2008.
Susan Woodford, *The Parthenon, Cambridge Introduction to World History*, Cambridge University Press 1981.

This book is for older readers, but includes many wonderful close-up photographs of the Parthenon sculptures in the British Museum:
Ian Jenkins, *The Parthenon Sculptures in the British Museum*, British Museum Press 2007.

INDEX

Acropolis 4, 5, 19, 20, 34–35
Acropolis Museum 35
aegis 8
Athena 5, 8–9, 12, 13, 14, 15, 19, 20, 31
Athens 5, 6, 12, 19, 34–35
athletes 18, 19

cattle 20, 22-23
carving the frieze 16–17
cavalry 23, 24–25
centaurs 10, 11
chariots 14, 23, 26–27
chryselephantine statue 8
churches 5, 34
colour 24–25
crane 7

democracy 6

Erechtheum 4, 20

frieze 16–17, 22–23, 24–25, 26–27
  28–29, 30–31, 32–33

gods 19, 22, 30–31
gold 5, 8

Hephaistos 8, 14, 30, 31
hoplite 26
horsemen 24–25
horses 15, 16, 24–25, 27

ivory 8–9

Lapiths 10
Lord Elgin 34, 35

marble 6, 10, 16
metopes 10–11

mosques 5, 34
musicians 28

Panathenaic Festival 18–19, 20, 22, 26, 30
Parthenon 4–5, 6–7, 10, 16, 20, 32–33, 34–35
pediments 12–13, 14–15
peplos 19, 20, 21, 31
Propylaea 4, 5, 20
Perikles 6, 24
Pheidias 8
Poseidon 12, 13, 31

statues of Athena 5, 8–9, 20, 31

temples on the Acropolis 4–5, 9, 20, 34

worshippers 5, 28–29

Zeus 14, 15, 19, 30